HyperChange

A Scheme of Consciousness

Preface

Scheme of Consciousness

When people write books there are usually so many steps. Edit this, check that, get a publisher, promo whatever ... etc.

Fuck it. Why not try something new?

I'm writing a book in less than a month. From start to finish. No one will read it until I self-publish it. No editor, no proofreader, no outside opinions, no influence, no hype, just me and HyperChange.

Why do this?

I want to show you how I think about the world with no filter. All of the processes in old-school publishing are just censors of authors work and ideas.

This is pure. This is real. Flaws exposed. It's all part of the art. Writing this book is like painting for me. Just letting the ideas flow to capture my passion at a single moment in time.

This means a cheaper book, faster publishing time, and the ability for me to move onto my next project. If you're not OK with grammatical errors or this philosophy, read something else. There are millions of books done the boring way already.

I call this new form of writing a *Scheme of Consciousness*.

It's a freestyle. In book form. It's art. This is a new era. I want to start a new genre.

It could totally flop and ruin my reputation. Or it could inspire my peers to think about writing in a new way and catalyze hundreds of books in this style. Or likely, something in-between :)

The world needs more out of the box, break the rules shit.

Things are changing faster than ever. Raw authenticity wins in this new digital era. This is a bet on that.

I hope this book leaves you with more questions than answers.

To the HyperChange subscribers - this book is for you.

Also I owe the biggest Thank You - Huge shoutout to my parents, lil sis, extended family, homies, mentors, teachers, and everybody else who has helped me scheme on all my crazy ideas through the years. This book would've never happened without you :) Also big thanks to Leo, Alex, jfilchê and Ri for reading this through at a moment's notice and giving me crucial last minute ideas.

My Investing Journey

I'm 24 as I type this. Am half Italian (mom), and half New Englander (dad). I grew up in Seattle and my parents are nerdy scientists. Moved to New York in 2011 to attend NYU and study finance. But that's the boring stuff.

My investing journey began in early 2008, when I was 15. Almost 10 years ago. I've easily put in 10,000+ hours learning about markets, but still feel like a total newb.

The first stock I bought was Sony. In 2008 nobody had HD TVs yet, but it was clear they were the future. The quality was a major step up, and they kept getting more affordable. I thought everybody was going to buy a new TV and upgrade (to watch the Superbowl of course, or that's why my Dad and I wanted to).

Then the recession happened and Sony crashed. But even if it didn't, TVs are a pretty commoditized business, so I doubt it would've been a great investment anyway.

Regardless, that got me hooked. The lightbulb went off. Stocks aren't just numbers on a computer screen, they are pieces of ownership in the businesses we interact with everyday.

Around the same time, Uncle Roli bought me *The Snowball* Warren Buffett's biography. By my sophomore year in high school I was waking up at 6:15 everyday to check the market and start trading. Whether it was flipping penny stocks, buying options on the silver bubble, or searching for the next Apple (ending up being Tesla), everyday was like Christmas. There was always another a financial theory to unwrap.

The more I learned about the stock market, finance and economics, the more passionate I became.

I quickly began to realize the important of money in our capitalist society. This is how the world works. This is how things change. This is how you can make a difference.

But believe it or not, I wasn't hooked on getting rich. I wanted the derivative; power & influence.

Not on some greedy shit. On some Robin Hood shit. Heist the fucking game, make billions, and give it back to the people.

There are so many problems the world needs to address. Fixing these with the brute force of unlimited, unrestrained capital, seemed like the most efficient method of personally instilling societal progress and making an impact.

To this day, I don't think politicians are the leaders of the free world. In fact, I believe their power continues wane by the day.

For better or worse, private sector wealth wields enormous and growing influence. Lobbying is institutionalized bribery. It's not a perfect system, but money (for the most part) allows individuals and corporations to either ignore the law, or change it.

In a utopia, government would iron out these issues, and become a fairer, more democratized platform. But I wasn't going to wait for that to happen.

It wasn't long before I figured out that hedge fund managers were the highest paid people in the world, with the top performers making billions of dollars in a single year.

I thought - I'm going to do that too. Get really rich investing, while simultaneously learning how to identify, run, and engage with successful businesses. A hybrid of wealth creation and education.

Long story short - I kept investing, and started blogging about stocks on Seeking Alpha in my senior year of high school. With that on my resume, during my Freshman year at NYU I got connected with a startup that helped students set up the infrastructure needed to manage small amounts of money. I raised $20,000 from the founder of the startup, my homie, and my mom. This was the closest thing to an investment fund that 19 year-old me could pull off.

In a 25 month period (July 2012 - August 2014) my investors made an 81% return, compared to 46% for the S&P 500 (assuming dividends reinvested). The majority of these gains came from ... you guessed it, Tesla (we bought in at $29).

This, combined with continued blogging on Seeking Alpha gave me the confidence and resume to step my shit up. One day I got an email from an investor named Sam (name changed), who liked my writing and wanted help doing stock research.

One thing led to another, and about a year later, Sam decided to give me $500,000 of his capital to invest in a portfolio of small-cap companies. I was 21.

Sam is the best investor I know. Most of what I learned

about interviewing management teams, thinking long-term and understanding business models, came from him.

But that's not what I admire most about him. He's so humble, genuine, friendly, and positive ... I almost think it's a shame more people don't know who he is. The world needs more people like Sam to get loud with their ideas.

Sorry I'm getting sidetracked. Getting $500,000 to manage was a dream come true. I had a mentor who was helping me and wanted me to grow. I was learning more than ever. Having his connections and capital allowed me to have 100+ 1x1 meetings with different CEOs of companies across all sectors. By my senior year at NYU I was routinely missing class to go to investment conferences, analyst days, and tune into earnings calls.

At the time, school was boring and a joke. I felt like I was killing it in the real world and didn't need to listen to professors who weren't. This was the naive cocky asshole in me, and I'm glad I started fucking up because of my egotistical attitude.

After I graduated in May 2015, I started managing the portfolio for Sam full-time. After a year, I felt like I was at a dead end. Working alone got lonely. I realized that I didn't want to sit behind a computer all day, keeping my best ideas to myself just to profit from them. There was an emptiness to it.

On top of that, my performance was lagging the Russell 2000 and overall inspiration was waning. It wasn't as easy to keep crushing the market as I thought it would be. Go figure.

It was time for a change. I needed to shake shit up.

While I was munching on a salad at Sweetgreen arguing about food stocks with an investing buddy, we started talking to two startup employees sitting next to us. They were in the food business, and within two weeks I had my first 9-5.

It was cool. I learned a lot working on a team. But also realized that management and I didn't share any of the same values. In late 2016 after 4 months on the job, I started pulling a GaryVee. Would do the 9-5, then go straight home and start working on content for HyperChange. It was a grind.

By February 2017, shit was hitting the fan at work. A $5M funding round was botched and only $500K was raised. With the company losing money and not much in the bank, about half of the employees were laid off, including me.

I had a little bit of money saved up, and decided to bet on myself and go all in.

My work in finance wasn't done.

HyperChange TV

Pouring your passion into something and making it public is really scary.

Your opening yourself up to criticism, scrutiny and judgement.

I've never worked at a bank or any kind of financial firm. I'm a rōnin. Self-taught on the internet and by a handful of key mentors.

The smartest financial minds my age are not creating content. They are working for banks, hedge funds, venture capital firms and tech companies. In the financial world making your views publicly available for critique and analysis is so taboo. What if you're wrong? You'll never get hired again!!! Everybody's decisions about their public statements are guided by fear. Nobody's on the offense.

With brightest people silent, the opportunity to openly publish my research is too good to ignore.

Have you ever watched CNBC? The analysis is stale, boring, filled with fallacies, and frankly toxic for anyone trying to educate themselves about financial markets. Why do you think the average viewer is 50+. Millennials and Gen Z aren't buying it.

Pundits, experts, newsletters and talking-heads from the old school financial media, will tell you they have all the answers. They can simultaneously predict what every stock will do tomorrow, while nonchalantly understanding the nuance of every macroeconomic trend. Sorry, I'm calling bullshit.

This "know it all" mentality is the exact reason they are failing. Nobody fully understands financial markets. The prevailing theories governing asset prices are all fluid and likely to be disrupted in perpetuity.

The second you think you know it all, is the second you've lost.

HyperChange is founded on this principle. I want every episode to leave you with more questions than answers. Get you to think more. Appreciate the complexity of the issues we discuss.

Unfortunately, the lack of quality financial analysis, combined with no education about taxes, stocks, or personal finance in school, has left my peers stranded. The level of financial illiteracy is astonishing, and I didn't see it improving. I'd bet 98% of Americans can't articulate the correlation between share price and market capitalization.

This is a real problem. How do we expect the populace to make informed decisions about laws and governance, without understanding the economic implications of their decisions?

The bigger the problem, the bigger the opportunity.

HyperChange TV is the financial show I think is missing. It's not the silver bullet by any means, but I think it makes learning accessible. I want to show people its OK to be wrong. It's OK to have new ideas. It's OK not to know it all.

Maybe it's crazy, but I think that's exactly what Wall

St needs - A kid in his bedroom reading SEC filings till 4am, making crazy predictions about the future of technology and finance. By documenting my journey of learning about the stock market, I want to help others along theirs.

Every other industry has had its "we just got fucked by the kid in the hoodie moment." Wall St is next.

So I started making YouTube videos. Just talking about my ideas on investing, and mostly Tesla. It was fun, and to my surprise, people were actually watching. So I kept pushing.

One day my buddy Omid came up with a new series idea called *Moonshot Monday*.

Pitch a moonshot buyout, partnership or just any crazy tech/business idea in a 5-10 minute episode. These pitches would not only include the business rationale and financial analysis, but offer clear evidence it was fiscally feasible and accretive to both parties.

In March 2017 me and Kevin (my homie and HyperChange's Creative Director) made "*Amazon Should Buy Whole Foods*." This was Moonshot Monday #4.

On June 16th, I woke up to texts from people I hadn't talked to in months, my Twitter was blowing up, jfilchê was calling me nonstop ...

It fucking happened. Amazon announced they were buying Whole Foods. Wall St was shocked. The business world was rocked. HyperChange and Scott Galloway were among a handful people who were lucky enough to see this coming. The stocks of Walmart, Costco, Target, Kroger and Supervalu fell between 4-12% the same day [10].

Somebody posted our video on Reddit/r/videos and somehow it took off, and remained in the top 3 for a day or two (and got nearly 100,000 views). This boosted the channel's subscribers from ~800 to 3K. But it wasn't about the growth, it was more than that. We were right.

We saw a $14B acquisition coming that will go down as the most transformative move in Amazon's history. We did it with no help. No paid research. No MBAs. Just two homies, a laptop, a camera and a vision for the future.

It's a real-world example of HyperChange. This would have never been possible before.

The little guy was one step ahead of Wall St.

Amazon+Whole Foods gave me the confidence to double down. Sell half my Tesla stock, cash out of Bitcoin and bootstrap HyperChange. I've been working my ass off ever since.

As I type this, I just sold the remainder of Bitcoin (more on this later), and have bought myself 6 months of burn for HyperChange. It feels like the universe has given me a second chance. When I originally started going full-time on HyperChange, Bitcoin was under $1K. For the past 12 months I've been strategically liquidating and sold most of my Bitcoin over $13K (20X+ from my original investment). Without this cash infusion I would've had to get a sidehustle (7-11 clerk, barista, waiter, dishwasher, babysitting job) months ago.

The two things (Tesla & Bitcoin) my professors, mentors, homies, the experts and pretty much the whole damn world thought were a joke and mistake to invest in ... were ironically the best investments I've ever made. Between both, I've made thousands of dollars, enabling me to fund my own startup out of pocket. Fuck you Wall St.

Now I'm going all in on improving the quality of my videos, making more creative content, pushing the envelope further, and building HyperChange into what I think it has the potential to be. The intersection of finance, economics, entrepreneurship & sustainability is something millions of people care about. Or should. I think it's partially my job to make sure this happens.

There's also a selfish motive behind HyperChange. I want to learn. I want to have people that are a lot smarter than me tell me I'm wrong, and explain why. Open sourcing my ideas has allowed this to happen. I owe so much to the people who watch my videos and give their input and advice. The connections I've made in the HyperChange community will last a lifetime, and are allowing me to learn more, faster, than I ever thought possible. Thank you HyperChangers.

Beyond educating and explaining my ideas/theories about finance and investing, HyperChange has a broader mission. Inspiring.

By watching me build HyperChange from the ground up, I want to show my subscribers that they can do it too. Bet on their passion. Work hard and do it by themselves. No industry approval needed.

There's never been a better time to be the scrappy underdog taking down the establishment, and I want to prove it.

HyperChange

Intro: The Bigger The Problem, The Bigger The Opportunity

WTF is HyperChange?

Literally, a word I made up.

Figuratively, I would describe it as the current economic era we are living in.

Life is getting weird. We talk to speakers with blue lights (Alexa), take selfies with Pikachu filters (Snapchat), tell kids to get into cars with strangers (Uber), and have strangers sleep in our houses (Airbnb). And don't even get me started on where dating apps are going (artificial intelligence algorithms determining who we mate with) ...

Things that were inconceivable years ago, are now social norms. The next 50 years of humanity (and maybe more) will be defined by this perpetually accelerating disruption.

We are living in HyperChange.

The backbone of this phenomena is rapid advances in technology.

Moore's law is enabling a data explosion. Software is eating the world. The internet is allowing frictionless communication and content distribution. We all have supercomputers in our pockets. We are living in a sci-fi movie and it's only going to get crazier, faster.

Among this disruption lies incredible opportunity, across every industry, in every geography.

Is this a good thing? Yes. Sure technology could kill us (robots, AI, looking at our phones, etc), but it's also the only chance we've got at survival.

We Need To Fix A Lot Of Shit Fast

There are almost 8 billion people on the planet today. By 2050 there will be almost 10 billion.

When imagining a future historian's take on the 21st century, I struggle to comprehend how we will be remembered.

Will this era will be looked upon as an independent creative renaissance where technological advancement, immense wealth creation and social progress pioneer us into an exciting multi-planetary future?

OR

Will this era be looked upon as a parabolic increase of materialistic gluttony, pollution, ramping ignorance, and a failure to govern with an eye towards our future, that ultimately results in our self-inflicted demise?

As of now we are teetering on the precipice of both outcomes. The point is, we are at a critical juncture in human history.

I'm equally scared shitless, and excited as fuck. You should be too.

Why Are We Ignoring Negative Externalities?

The biggest flaw in our current version of democratic capitalism (& society in general) is we do not tax negative externalities.

When you fill up your car with oil, you're not paying for the pollution you emit. When you get a latte at Starbucks, you don't pay for throwing away your cup.

Science is quickly proving nearly every industry and institution that built the US (and world) economy up until now, is unsustainable.

What do I mean by unsustainable? If we keep up our current trajectory of consumption, the planet's ability to foster a biome that humans can live in, will be a thing of the past. If its 100 years, 200 or 1,000, I'm not sure.

But I don't think it's worth finding out.

Whether it's oil, natural gas, the internal combustion engine, coal, factory farming, monoculture crops, pesticide and fertilizer use, healthcare, social security, the military industrial complex, fast-fashion, beauty, excessive consumption, waste, or forced child labor. You name it. If an industry is making a lot of money today, it's probably fucking up the planet.

To give you some idea what I'm talking about ....

We are on track to have more plastic in the ocean than fish (by weight) by 2050 [1].

50% of the world's species (animals) will be facing extinction by the end of this century [2].

Carbon dioxide (CO_2) in the Earth's atmosphere is above 400ppm, the highest it's been in 800,000 years [3].

2017 was the US' third hottest year on record (based on

123 years of data), the other two were 2012 and 2016 [4].

Rainforests cover 6% of our planet's landmass and produce 40% of the Earth's oxygen [5], and they will completely vanish in 100 years at the current rate of deforestation [6].

Worldwide sea levels have risen ~8 inches in the past 100 years, and the pace of this rise is accelerating [7].

The average American produces 4.4 pounds of trash every single day [8].

That's all scary, and what's even scarier is these stats are only scratching the surface. I could've listed 100 more, but you get the point. Start Googling.

I'm not a scientist by any means (so take my analysis with a big grain of salt).

But I am a citizen of Earth, who thinks we need to be exponentially more thoughtful about the impact of our everyday decisions and the negative externalities that come with them.

Nobody's perfect, and I myself am guilty of perpetuating

all of these atrocities, but understanding this is the important first step towards finding solutions.

What's so frustrating about policy makers lack of focus on this, is that taxing negative externalities is objectively rational in the long-term. It's like an ultra high-interest credit card loan we are taking out on nature. Sure, we don't pay for shit upfront, but it will fuck us later.

This is the biggest thing that governments need to fix in our lifetime. Otherwise the burden will be on individuals to price in negative externalities themselves. For some reason I doubt that will be as effective.

What if we taxed oil companies based on incremental GHG emissions and used the revenue to subsidize electric transport & renewable energy?

What if we taxed plastic and used the money to fund education about the environment and cleaned up our oceans?

Trash

Go anywhere on the planet and look at all the garbage. Plastic bags, soda cans, wrappers, cigarette butts, beer bottles, etc. It's all manmade, recent and nobody cares. How is this not an abomination?

Our respect for the natural world has fallen drastically in the past few centuries. We're out of touch.

We've focused on growth and economic expansion at all costs, leaving our planet by the wayside.

Reversing this trajectory of consumption and waste will not be easy. But it is going to be necessary if we want to avoid Idiocracy.

The Bigger The Problem, The Bigger The Opportunity

It's difficult to understate the urgency at which our capitalist infrastructure needs to be utterly transformed from the inside out for our species to survive beyond the next few centuries.

We need to transition off fossil fuels and dramatically reduce the untethered consumption patterns that have been increasingly ingrained in our society. But those are just the first steps.

Sorry the beginning of this book has been so dark. I promise it's getting brighter.

At the end of the day, I'm incredibly hopeful.

We all have the chance to play instrumental roles in permanently altering the habits of society and pivot humanity towards a sustainable future.

Companies that solve these challenges are waiting to be built.

Entrepreneurs who create products and services that disrupt the status quo are waiting to be born.
We desperately need HyperChange. And you have the chance to be a part of it. If that doesn't motivate you, I don't know what will.

HyperChange

Industries, Trends & The Future

Bitcoin, Ethereum & The Blockchain

"Gold is a shiny rock, Money is green paper, and Bitcoin is a chunk of code."

"Software is eating the world, Blockchain is eating software."
    -Alexander Tsankov

Part of the reason I wanted to write this book so quickly and get it out, is because things are changing so fast. Bitcoin and cryptoassets are a perfect example of this.

What's The Dollar?

The prevailing bear thesis I hear on Bitcoin is that it's worthless. No inherent value.

Well what's the inherent value of the US Dollar? We got off the Gold standard in 1971.
(hint: It's just green paper)

Bitcoin may go to shit, but you should at least know that what's backing it up is the same thing propping up the US Dollar.

Trust.

The only reason you are OK with Dollars and not Bitcoin is because everybody accepts dollars. You *trust* that they will retain their value and be accepted as a medium of exchange.

The US Dollar might be the world's biggest cult.

I don't see any reason why trust in a cryptoasset can't rival a central bank's in my lifetime.

If one thing in history is constant, it's that mediums of exchange and stores of value are constantly being disrupted. So why is assuming that the status quo (US Dollar) will last in perpetuity so normal?

<u>It's A Bubble Right?</u>

It's easy to label anything that's rapidly rising in value as a bubble and capture the near-term praise of being viewed as a shrewd skeptic. This attitude is very in vogue in the financial media.

We could be witnessing a bubble, or we could be witnessing one of the most disruptive technologies in modern finance go mainstream. You tell me.
The recent news of random microcaps (Long Island Iced Tea, Eastman Kodak, Riot Blockchain, etc) including the

word blockchain in their business model and going up 5-10X overnight, is only one side of the story. Sure, it's the sign of a frothy market, and irrational exuberance, but we saw the same thing happen with the internet bubble of the early 2000s.

Yes, there was a period where tech stocks were over-valued, and investing in them was a let down. But, the overarching vision of the internet changing the world forever, could not have been more accurate.

In most cases, bubbles are a natural cyclical prerequisite for hyperdisruptive technologies.

I think we are seeing a similar phenomena with cryptoassets and the blockchain. The disruptive potential is real, and will change the world, but near-term asset prices are probably vastly inflated by greedy speculators.

Blockchain, The Tech Behind Cryptoassets

Bitcoin and Ethereum may not last. But the technology behind them will.

It's called blockchain. I've only met a couple people who seem to fully understand it. I'm still just getting my feet wet learning about it, but from what I can tell, the potential is staggering. Monumental. Trillions.

At its most basic level, the blockchain is a spreadsheet. A list of transactions. What makes it special is everybody confirms the same transactions, and they are transparently available for everybody to see.

This has the ability to commoditize trust, and decentralize many of the functions offered by central banks, Wall St, and the world's largest corporations.

It's worth learning about.

How Do You Value Cryptoassets?

The short answer is, nobody knows. And that's the fun part.

I like things that I don't understand. It pushes me to

learn, get uncomfortable and compound my investing knowledge. That's why I originally bought Bitcoin. The idea was so fascinating, out of this world, and too complex for me too grasp. I didn't bet my life savings on it, but I put in enough to move the needle if it ever 20+ baggered (it did).

Sure, there is no P/E ratio, earnings, or book value for financial nerds to value these cryptoassets, but they aren't stocks. This is an entirely new asset class that is not going away.

Just because you don't understand something's value, doesn't mean it doesn't have any.

Valuing cryptoassets is still an infantile school of thought. Chris Burniske is probably the leader. He's worth a follow.

My basic investment/valuation rationale on Bitcoin is pretty simple. It's digital gold. A global decentralized store of value that isn't controlled by a single entity and has a finite supply. Basically a hedge against inflation and g-check on the central bank fiat system.

Here's a back of the napkin calculation to show you how I think about valuing cryptoassets:

The value of all the gold in the world is $7.5T. There are only 21M Bitcoin that will ever be created. So, if Bitcoin fulfills this vision of digital gold its network value would be in same ballpark, putting its price per coin at ~$357,000 (7.5T/21M).

Storytime

In business school, Bitcoin was a joke. (that's part of the reason I thought business school was a joke).

Especially to all my professors. Except one. He was an awesome VC that taught an entrepreneurship class. He had a conspiracy theory that the government created Bitcoin in 2008, at the peak of the Great Recession, incase shit REALLY hit the fan. It was a backup if the Dollar collapsed.

True or not, this crazy theory got me hooked on Bitcoin and eventually the Blockchain. It was 2013 and Bitcoin was at $30.

Satoshi Nakamoto

It's estimated that Bitcoin's founder Satoshi Nakamoto owns ~980,000 coins. No one knows who he is. But he's going to be the richest guy on the planet if Bitcoin crosses ~$100,000 (depending on how fast Amazon stock keeps rising).

What dystopia are we living? We're one more Bitcoin bull-run away from an anonymous cryptocurrency founder being by far the richest man on Earth. And Donald Trump is President.

You tell me we aren't living in a Black Mirror episode.

If cryptoassets continue to be a valid asset class, an entirely new generation of wealth will be created. It's revenge of the nerds 2.0 and Satoshi will be king.

<u>Pollution</u>

One of the dirty secrets of cryptoassets is the amount of energy required to run their respective networks.

The backbone of every cryptoasset is a decentralized network of server farms all around the world, performing the cryptography tasks required to validate the block-chain. At its current stage, this process (across almost every cryptoasset) is excruciatingly energy intensive.

If the rate of energy consumption by these networks does not decline radically in the near future, the entire disruptive premise of the blockchain will fall by the wayside.

The good news is smart people are working around the clock to solve this technological challenge. I'm hopeful.

Why I Sold Bitcoin (Digital Gold) & Bought Ethereum (Digital Oil)

Speaking of smart people working around the clock, I think Ethereum is the most fascinating cryptoasset.

I recently (last night, 1/11/17) sold all the rest of my Bitcoin & Bitcoin Cash (minus 0.01 BTC as a sentimental momento), and now Ethereum is my only material cryptoasset position. To be clear most of my Bitcoin gains are going to fund HyperChange, but still, I put some into Ethereum.

Here's why.

Bitcoin is breaking. The network hasn't been able to scale beyond processing much more than 350K transactions per day since late 2016. The average fee per transaction hasn't dropped below $20 since mid December 2017. And the Bitcoin Cash fork freaked me out. The developer mindshare of the Bitcoin community is divided, there's bad blood, and I think that's a major impediment to progress.

Beyond that, the bull case of Ethereum results in a far larger potential network value than that of Bitcoin. As I type this the network value of Bitcoin is $234B, and the network value of Ethereum is $120B.

If Bitcoin's $7.5T digital gold endgame is sexy, the Ethereum endgame of *digital oil* is even sexier.

It's not just a decentralized store of value (see stable-coins being built on the Ethereum blockchain), it's how we execute smart contracts in the digital economy. Put simply, it's how shit actually gets done. In a bull-case, this is the backbone of Web 3.0. It's a platform for decentral-ized applications (dapps) to run on. You're not betting on Ethereum, you're betting on what can be built on top of it. It's like the iOS app store, but with a much grander, decentralized vision.

Sure, a lot of other cryptoassets could claim to com-pete with Ethereum and build a similar smart contracts platform, but I think it's clear who's winning (at least for now).

Ethereum was founded and is currently led by Vitalik Buterin, one of today's most intriguing intelligent fanatics. He's 23, a Thiel Fellowship award winner, and quickly becoming a worshipped philosopher in the cryptoasset community.

Having a known leader that can resolve issues, guide strategy, and lead the Ethereum developer community like a nimble startup, is a major advantage over Bitcoin, whose founder remains anonymous and silent.

That's all great, but what really matters is Vitalik and the Ethereum Foundation are executing. The Ethereum blockchain was processing 45K transactions per day entering 2017, and now that number is consistently over 1M, and continues to scale rapidly. That means the network is already capable of processing 3X what Bitcoin can.

In the past 12 months Ethereum has leapfrogged Bitcoin in capacity and the gap continues to widen.

But even Ethereum isn't quite ready for primetime yet.

To put things in context, Visa's network processes about 150M transactions per day. Ethereum at 1M+ is still a drop in the bucket. But it's not about where we're at today, it's about where we're headed. Vitalik and his team continue to work on some of the world's most advanced cryptography in order to tackle this scaling challenge. As the network continues to grow rapidly, the progress is transparently evident.

Going from 45K to 1M in 2017 was a 22X year over year increase. If Ethereum continues at this rate, we will be at 22M/day at the end of 2018, and 484M/day by the end of 2019. This is just a back of the napkin extrapolation, but you get the point. In 2-3 years this thing could dwarf Visa and be tackling much bigger challenges. This is the multi-trillion Dollar bull case for Ethereum.

Risks

If you're not prepared to lose all of your money, you shouldn't invest in cryptoassets.

If Bitcoin starts crashing, it will get ugly. A pullback of 80% or more would not surprise me. It's happened before. In 2013, Bitcoin fell from over $1000 to below $200 in just 8 months.

In these scenarios, exchanges (like Coinbase) will freeze and lock your assets, creating even more panic and accentuating the downward spiral. It'll be a crypto bank run.

Bitcoin won't be the only thing that gets hit. My guess is all of the cryptoassets will fall in lockstep if a crash starts happening.

It's important to be excited about cryptoassets. But it's equally as important to accept they could be worthless at any moment in time. Without this mindset, you're setting yourself up for disappointment.

The Internet At Scale

It's hard to fathom how much opportunity the internet creates.

The internet has taken the shackles off the distribution of content and ideas. It's commoditizing knowledge faster than ever before.

In the grand scheme of history, we are still in the infancy of witnessing the profound impact global connectivity will have on our civilization. We're 20 years in to the modern internet. Maybe less.

The internet is exposing the truth in an unprecedented fashion. This is exactly what we need to accelerate HyperChange and help us uncover the negative externalities that corporations are incentivized to keep quiet.

Creators & The Decentralization of Brand Equity

Individuals now have more power than brands.

The top 5 most followed Twitter accounts are people. Not brands or companies. Same with the top 5 most followed Instagram accounts and YouTube channels.

Creators are a new *tour de force* in media that we've never seen before. They are platform agnostic, and boast followings that old school networks could not begin to comprehend.

Social networks like YouTube, Instagram, Snapchat and Facebook are enabling individuals to create and distribute content, gain a following, monetize it, globally, for free.

We are going through a massive power shift in the media industry. Cable companies and network conglomerates are in denial of the attention they are losing on a daily basis.

The floodgates are open. Beyond the proliferation of smartphones, professional cameras are being commoditized at an astonishing rate. Video editing software continues to improve. Any advice from what camera to buy, how to learn editing software, to how to light a set, can be found on YouTube in minutes.

While this is happening ... Tech companies like Amazon, Netflix, Facebook and Apple are rapidly scaling multi-billion dollar original content budgets. This is no coincidence.

YouTube and other social networks are quickly becoming the training ground for these bigger VC-style entertainment dollars.

Mark Zuckerberg has called this the Golden Era of video. He's right. We are witnessing an explosion of unfiltered creativity.

There has never been a better time to be a content creator. Own your art and distribute it yourself. Nobody can stop you.

The Future of Food

Our food system is a fucking mess.

Agriculture is one of the biggest global emitters of

greenhouse gases. It's the hidden juggernaut ushering in climate change.

It's the reason we're cutting down the Amazon, causing thousands of species to go extinct, and more broadly destroying the natural beauty of Earth at an astonishing rate.

I know that you think driving electric is important (so do I), and it is, but what you eat is arguably worth even more scrutiny.

Livestock and animal product consumption is by far the biggest culprit of agriculture's pollutive nature.

I don't think going vegan is the complete answer, or going vegetarian (I could be dead wrong), although these are important steps in the right direction. I think we just need to rebalance our diets. The masterminds behind standardizing dietary guidelines, food education and policy, are the world's largest food companies.

This new industrialized system has dramatically reduced the accountability of the farmers and firms that grow our food. Nobody knows where their eggs came from or who raised the chickens anymore.
Corporate incentives are aligned to sell more products,

not create a more sustainable supply chain. Let alone get you the healthiest and most nutritious food. They don't care about you. They care about profit.

But there's a lot of hope.

I'm a huge believer that we are in the early stages of witnessing a multi-decade transition, from an industrialized-era food system of making things cheaper and faster, to a decentralized system of micro-artisans.

Avocado toast, craft beer, $6 lattes, quinoa, salads, call it what you want. Consumers aren't just getting gourmet, they are getting smarter.

<u>Where Food Comes From</u>

If there's any hope for saving the food system, education will be the catalyst of progress.

It's not that consumers want to ruin the environment. It's that they don't know they are doing it.
The more I learn about where my food comes from, the more I care and the more informed purchasing decisions I make.

Clean Meat

This is exactly the kind of technology that makes me excited for the future.

Impossible Foods is recreating the burger from the ground up with 100% plant-based vegan ingredients. But it's not your average veggie burger. It looks, tastes, and bleeds like meat. Founded by a Stanford professor, they have already raised $250M from people like Bill Gates and are making millions of pounds of the 'Impossible Burger.' The future is coming, and fast.

Other startups like Memphis Meats are pioneering even more complex versions of burgers without the cows, by trying to grow animal stem cells in test tubes. This technology also has the potential to get us the burgers we love, with a fraction of the environmental impact.

And burgers aren't the only thing getting disrupted. These startups (and many more) have ambitions to recreate all types of livestock products more sustainably, while vastly improving animal welfare.

Indoor Farming: Gigagreenhouses

In 10 years, you'll tap a button on your Amazon app and

a robot will immediately begin harvesting your lettuce on the 28th floor of a massive greenhouse. A drone will pick this up, and fly it to you within 30 minutes.

Gigagreenhouses aren't some future far-off technology. They are here, scaling rapidly, and being funded by hundreds of millions of dollars of the world's smartest capital (see AeroFarms, Plenty, etc).

I'm talking about multi-story, hydroponic, software-controlled, LED lit, skyscrapers that grow fruits and vegetables.

This new tech-centric farming method has several key advantages over old-school agriculture.

It reduces food miles and supports local economies (we can build these near cities). It can be 10-100X more efficient per square foot (you can go vertical). It uses 90% less water (you can recycle, it is a closed loop). No fertilizers are put into the environment. It can grow food year round. And changing weather patterns from climate change can't hurt yields.

Why is now the time for gigagreenhouses?

The biggest cost input is energy (heating, cooling, lighting, fans, etc). If you're burning coal to run these green-houses it doesn't make much sense. If you're using solar panels and wind turbines, we're getting somewhere.

As batteries and solar panels continue to get cheaper (thanks Elon), the economics and sustainability profile of gigagreenhouses are getting more attractive by the day.

Beyond the commercial gigagreenhouses, hydroponic technology scales down to the micro. We're talking mini-farms in houses, schools and communities across America. Empowering people to grow their own food will do wonders for food security, and awakening society to the nuances of the whole system.

We are too far removed from the food that we eat. And it's only getting worse. Indoor farming can help reverse this trend.

Moonshot Monday: Amazon Buys Gotham Greens

Gotham Greens is an exciting example of HyperChange. They are reimagining the urban landscape by building hydroponic greenhouses on unused rooftops. They have a partnership with Whole Foods, and built a farm on top of a store. It's partially powered by solar panels that offer shade over the parking lot. I've been there, it's in Brooklyn (of course).

In total Gotham Greens runs 4 rooftop farms. According to their website, each location is getting significantly more efficient than the last. The original location in Greenpoint, Brooklyn (built in 2011) can grow 6.7lbs of produce/square-foot/year, the newest one in Chicago (built in 2015) can grow 100lbs of produce/square-foot/year.

They grow different kinds of gourmet lettuces, basil, tomatoes and even make pesto, year round. These products are sold directly below on the shelves of Whole Foods. There are 0 food miles involved in this operation.

On the shelf next to Gotham Greens products, are Whole Foods 365 private label branded lettuces. They are the same price. If you check the back of the 365 lettuces' label it says they are distributed from a Whole Foods facility in Austin, Texas. That's 1,700 miles from Brooklyn.

I don't think shipping trucks full of lettuce across the country that require constant refrigeration is a great long-term solution to our greens supply chain. Even if they are using a renewably powered Tesla Semi truck.

Beyond transport costs and emissions, this system means food that's far less fresh and therefore less nutritious and lower quality.

Now that Amazon owns Whole Foods, they can think long-term, invest in the future and leverage access to unlimited amounts of capital.

My pitch - Buy Gotham Greens for a $Bil or two, build rooftop farms on the majority of the 460+ Whole Foods stores, and then start building additional capacity on the roofs of Amazon distribution centers. Amazon could take Gotham Greens' technology and scale it to replace all of Whole Foods 365 lettuce, and eventually expand into other crops and disrupt the entire produce industry.

Given Amazon has clearly committed to selling food (and lots of it) by purchasing Whole Foods, they should vertically integrate. Grow the food. Dig the moat deeper. Buy Gotham Greens, or build out the infrastructure themselves. Just do it. The technology is ready for primetime, and the world needs it.

I don't think it's a coincidence Jeff Bezos' personal venture fund Bezos Expeditions is funding Plenty, a hydroponic farming startup very similar to Gotham Greens. The secret is out.

Do some good with all that power, Amazon. Buy Gotham Greens. If you're going to disrupt and dominate the food system, do it sustainably. If you don't, it won't be long before Walmart starts building farms on top of their stores.

The GMO Debate

I'm not against GMOs (Genetically Modified Organisms). I'm against the GMO industrial complex. Yes I'm talking about Monsanto.

It's not that I have a problem eating GMOs because I'm worried they will adversely affect my personal health (although it may, I'll let people smarter than me debate this).

I have a problem eating GMOs because I have a problem with the way that 99% of them are grown. Personally, it's not a health issue, it's an environmental issue.

Monsanto locks farmers into their proprietary seed and fertilizer ecosystem. Once you start using them, it's really hard to stop. It heavily incentivizes monocrop farming. It requires spraying massive amounts of pesticides that leach into the soil (and then our water supply) and ruin neighboring farms (who aren't using Monsanto products). None of this is part of a food system I support.

Travel

Airbnb has already done so much good, and they are just getting started.

Experiencing new cultures is cheaper and easier than ever before. Platforms like AirBnB (along with the internet in general) are making it easier to navigate new countries, explore new cities, and immerse yourself with locals. It's a game changer.

This is a perfect example of how technology is dramatically improving an aspect of life that can really move the needle on happiness.

Moonshot Monday: AirBnB Launches An Airline

The entire experience of getting to an airport, going through security and riding on a plane is ripe for disruption. It sucks. It's the biggest pain point to traveling, and therefore the biggest friction on AirBnB's addressable market of tourism.

AirBnB could either buy an airline (a reverse merger

with one that's already public would also be an IPO fast track #twobirdswithonestone), or just build its own from the ground up.

I'm talking create a new terminal. Better food. Cleaner. Cozier. More comfortable. Curate the entire experience from leaving your home, to stepping foot in somebody else's home, halfway across the world.

Fashion

I've started at least 3 t-shirt business that have all 'failed' in the eyes of society. But frankly, I'm just getting started. All of these failures will be the foundational building blocks of my success.

Clothes are an intimate expression of identity. They are personally curated art pieces we display for everybody to see.

They are the first impression (real world landing page) of your personal brand.

Whether it's 'I'm wearing sweatpants to be comfy and IDGAF what you think' or 'I'm wearing a Supreme t-shirt to hide my insecurity that I might not be cool' ... you're making a statement.

90% (probably more) of mainstream fashion brands profit on the back of cheap, forced labor and pollutive ingredients.

That's why starting a great t-shirt company is so hard. If you really want to do it right, you need to reinvent the whole supply chain.

Beyond using unsustainable raw ingredients, cheap t's with generic screen printed logos, priced depending on Instagram marketing prowess, is the depressing norm for being a trendsetting brand.

This is an industry with massive negative externalities we fail to appreciate. In many ways, it is the most poignant example of our excessive materialism.

The bigger the problem, the bigger the opportunity.

We are at an exciting inflection point in fashion, it needs to HyperChange.

It will. Startups (Modern Meadow, Remake, Allbirds) are already beginning to tackle some of the industry's biggest challenges.

Beyond drastically reducing the environmental footprint

of clothing production, we need to rethink our ideology surrounding clothing consumption. The amount of clothes people buy, accumulate, and collect is absurd. Closets full of clothes we never wear.

A way to fix this is foster a deeper connection between individuals and each piece of clothing they own. Make people appreciate, cherish, and maximize the utility of every product.

Self-Driving Cars

The hype on fully self-driving cars has been overdone in the near term. Even Elon Musk thinks we are at least 2-3 years away. I think we're a lot closer to 10 before fully self-driving cars become a mass market reality.

Either way. It's not a matter of if, but rather when. So let's get to the fun stuff.

The implications of autonomous vehicle technology go far beyond making Ubers cheaper.

Cites are designed with transportation first. Manhattan is a tiny, cramped island with 1.7 million people, and the only space where we don't have massive skyscrapers is where we allow a non-stop congestion of polluting cars to drive.

The entire real-estate ecosystem is in for a mega rebalancing.

Getting from A to B is a massive societal pain point that we blindly accept. Commuting for hours in traffic, standing (probably sweating) on a packed subway car, sitting on a dirty, bumpy bus ... if you're not walking to work, there's a good chance your commute sucks.

Parking lots will become irrelevant. Traffic will decrease. Commutes will become shorter and more pleasant. Driving will be much safer. There is a lot to be excited about here.

Transportation will look a lot different in 50 years. We are in the midst of two massive revolutions, electrification and autonomy. The opportunity has been deemed tantalizing enough for Apple, Google, Uber, Tesla (and many more) to throw billions of dollars at developing the technology behind this.

But it's not just cars that will go autonomous. Trucks, planes, trains, boats, you name it. It's coming to everything that carries goods or people.

Whether we're in flying cars or shooting through underground tunnels at 150mph, the future can't come fast enough.

Space

"You want to wake up in the morning and think the future is going to be great - and that's what being a spacefaring civilization is all about. It's about believing in the future and thinking that the future will be better than the past. And I can't think of anything more exciting than going out there and being among the stars."
      -Elon Musk

We are going to colonize Mars, and probably a lot sooner than you realize.

Elon's rocket company SpaceX, is targeting sending a cargo mission to Mars in 2022 and a manned mission to Mars in 2024 [9]. That's right, we are *less than a decade* away from sending people to Mars. Fucking epic.

Star Wars and Star Trek aren't just awesome fictional masterpieces. They are a preview of our multi-planetary future.

Humanity needs a cause to rally around. A future to get excited and inspired about. I think this is it.

Creating a branch of civilization on Mars will be the biggest power move we've made as a species ... ever.

A lot of people are frustrated by the assumed beef between billionaires Jeff Bezos and Elon Musk, but I love it.

They are fighting tooth and nail to be the first one to colonize space. Competition breeds innovation.

Jeff Bezos is already selling $1B worth of Amazon stock per year to fund his rocket company Blue Origin. Elon Musk will probably start doing the same to fund SpaceX when Tesla begins producing positive operating cash flow (my guess is 2019/2020).

The biggest breakthrough in this field has been reusable rocket technology. Prior to SpaceX, rockets were one and done. You launched it, cargo was delivered, then it crashed on into the ocean or blew up somewhere in space and that was it. Want to launch something else? Build a whole new rocket.

Elon Musk has redefined this entire equation. SpaceX

can now launch a rocket, deliver cargo and then re-land that same rocket on a drone ship in the ocean. After a quick refurbishment and refueling, it's ready to launch again.

This is a gamechanger.

Reusable rockets have the potential to drop the cost of a launch from hundreds of millions to $5M. More than an order of magnitude improvement.

With rapidly falling launch costs, the possibilities for what we can do in space continue to compound.

One example is SpaceX's proposed low-orbit satellite network that will provide internet everywhere on the planet (dubbed Starlink) and eventually enable communication between Earth and Mars.

Asteroid mining is another exciting tangential industry that reusable rockets enable. There is a finite amount of natural resources we can exploit on Earth. Eventually we'll need to tap into space to satiate our demand for raw materials. The company with the cheapest launch costs will have an edge here too.

Neuralink

If Elon Musk is right about one of his most futuristic projects, we are going to be living in a Black Mirror episode sooner rather than later.

Potentially a distant great grandson of the smartphone, embedded neurological devices will be the start of humanity going officially symbiotic with AI.

On its website, the Neuralink describes its technology as the following:

Neuralink is developing ultra high bandwidth brain-machine interfaces to connect humans and computers.

This is some scary shit. Basically your brain is directly tied to the internet and an artificial intelligence platform. The overarching premise of this bionic innovation is to protect us. Elon Musk fears that AI will become so powerful, our only chance at survival will be to integrate it into our own bodies.

So of course, he's creating a company to do just that. It's called Neuralink.

Beyond further commoditizing access to the knowledge of the internet, this will have immense social implications.

Recording every memory you ever experience, via all 5 senses and then storing it on the cloud (you think getting hacked now is a nightmare).

This is some unreal shit, and frankly I hope I die before these implants become the norm. Maybe that's the luddite in me ... regardless, it's important to understand where we're headed.

All The Rest

There's so much more. Genetics, biotech, physics, AI, and all the rest of the deep-tech I can't understand. It's moving at lightning speed. The amount of exciting cutting edge shit happening right now is epic. It's worth taking a step back to appreciate.

Even old school industries like painting, music, photography are all going through massive disruption in their own way.

Nothing is safe from HyperChange.

We Are At The Cusp Of A New Renaissance

Some thoughts on the future:

In the way that the Medici's, Borgia's, and Florence's elite funded a creative explosion in the arts and science 500 years ago, we are about to enter a parallel era with an order of magnitude more potential. An explosion of science and art.

We are already seeing the early stages. The Sergey Brins, Jeff Bezos, Elon Musks, Bill Gates, Warren Buffetts have compounded an absurd amount of money in their lifetimes. And they are probably going to keep getting richer until they die.

No pressure, but it's on the shoulders of these modern day Rockefellers to start funding the future.

Making definitive progress towards slowing the rate of climate change (saving us), implementing electronic voting systems (democratizing us), promoting equality socially and socioeconomically (leveling the playing field) ... these are a just a few of the critical issues that the morally conscious financiers and barons of our era have the opportunity to tackle.

I hope the next 100 years are as exciting as they have the potential to be.

People need to start living up to their creative potential. That's why Kanye West is so inspiring to me.

His music is vertically integrated (he can produce & rap), and therefore he can create his own unique sound and is completely authentic. Kanye can go 0 to 1. This is why he can (and has) pioneered entirely new genres of hip hop and music. Even his shows, he designs the set and crafts the visuals.

He's transferring this artistic touch to clothing with an Adidas partnership (where I can guarantee he's under-paid given his halo effect on the brand). Partnerships like this will only get more common in the future. Beyond that, he describes ambitions for architecture and more.

We need more Kanyes. We need more people funding Kanyes.

More public art, bigger scientific projects, more experiments, I don't know. Just start investing in creators.

The internet has made discovering today's most talented

artists instantaneous. We are all watching them make history in real time.

The reinventing of our infrastructure in the name of sustainability, opens the door to enormous creative opportunities.

Self-driving cars means the parking lots dominating the landscape of suburbia are suddenly a blank canvas. Micro-farms? Reforestation? Studio space? R&D labs? Massive statues? It's up to us.

Gigagreenhouses. These could glow purple, blue or red. Twist and and grow to the sky like beautiful food producing forests.

Going to Mars, living in space, exploring new planets.

There's so much opportunity to build an inspiring future.

HyperChange

Tesla & Amazon

Tesla

<u>Storytime</u>

In my Sophomore year of high school I was on the debate team, my partner was AJ. The topic of the year (or whatever prompt we had to debate) was proposing a solution to climate change.

We schemed on this for hours and eventually came up with an *epic* plan.

We were going to build massive genetically modified algae farms in the middle of the Arizona desert, to intake enormous amounts of greenhouse gases and then process that algae as biofuel, and create a more sustainable transportation system.

The idea had a million problems and we didn't have the first clue about the science, but we knew that a transportation system based on fossil fuels was bullshit.

Shortly after, I discovered Tesla. And realized Elon Musk had come up with a far better solution. Create the sexiest, fastest, most-long range electric cars on the planet and force going green on the world by making Tesla's products cooler and more practical than the internal combustion engine.

I thought... now that's a helluva fucking scheme. And I've been hooked on learning more about the company ever since.

This Is My favorite Company
(full disclosure I'm an Elon Musk fanboy and Tesla shareholder)

The biggest challenge we face as a collective humanity over the next century is not destroying the equilibrium of nature. Tesla is making more progress on this initiative than any other entity on the planet.

Elon Musk is quickly becoming living proof that one inspired leader can change the course of history.

I've been following Tesla for 10 years now and the progress has been nothing short of astounding.

In 2012, when Tesla first started selling its luxury sedan (The Model S), the consensus among the world's leading economists, analysts and experts was that the company would fail because electric vehicles (EVs) would never go mainstream.

Now I sit in 2018, and read headlines everyday about how all the major automakers are planning to electrify their entire car lineups as fast as possible.

EVs went from impossible to inevitable in half a decade. Thanks to Tesla.

Tesla combines Apple's detailed oriented product obsession and luxury brand status, with Amazon's growth at all costs vision-first fiscal engineering strategy. This is a powerful combination we've never seen before.

The amount of hate that Tesla gets in the media baffles me. I understand there is a structural incentive for people to cover every Tesla event with a negative slant if they are short the stock (AKA will profit if Tesla goes bankrupt).

But the skepticism, judgement and negativity seems to permeate far beyond that.

Do you not believe the world needs to transition off of fossil fuels? Does the incredible David vs Goliath story of a nobody-Silicon-Valley-startup single handedly taking down the oil-industrial complex not inspire you?

Whatever. The haters aren't worth my time.

Tesla currently sells 3 cars. The Model S ($70K+ luxury sedan), Model X ($70K+ luxury SUV), and Model 3 ($35K+ sedan).

Additionally, the company has announced plans to produce the Model Y ($35K+ SUV), Roadster 2.0 ($200K+ luxury sports car), Tesla Semi (all electric heavy duty truck) and eventually a pickup.

But Tesla isn't just making electric cars and trucks. The mission to accelerate the transition away from fossil fuels involves much bigger plans.

If we are all driving electric vehicles, we will need a lot more energy. Combine that with the fact that the majority of the US's power comes from coal, natural gas and oil, and you've got a major problem. Or opportunity, depending on who you ask.

A drastic increase in energy demand will require a sustainable way to produce and deliver that power. Enter Tesla Energy.

Tesla is building the world's largest battery factory in Nevada (the Gigafactory). Yes, this will pump out batteries for cars, but perhaps more importantly it will make batteries to store energy to power the rest of our lives.

Batteries are the missing link that allow the renewable energy sources we need to power our future (solar, wind, geothermal, tidal, etc), to be practical.

The sun isn't always shining and the wind isn't always blowing. To smooth out these intermittent power sources, you need batteries to store energy and deliver it when needed.

It's a whole ecosystem. Electric car in the garage, solar on your roof, and a battery tying it all together. That is why Tesla bought SolarCity. They want to sell you this package of complete sustainability. This trifecta is the fossil fuel killer.

As the costs of batteries and solar panels continue to drop, Tesla's renewable energy solutions are getting more competitive by the day. At this point, the momentum is irreversible.

We are going green and there's nothing you can do about it. Morals were great, but now economics are on Tesla's side too.

People will be studying Tesla and the multi-industry disruption it is catalyzing for hundreds of years into the future. The fact that we are witnessing it play out in real-time is beyond incredible.

Tesla is HyperChange.

The Investing Bull Case

The bull thesis is; Apple of cars. The high margin luxury status symbol that captures 10% of the industry's market share, and 90% of the profit.

But frankly the vision is bigger. Tesla extends beyond the consumer piece. Rebuilding the electric grid is a multi-trillion dollar opportunity that accompanies the EV revolution. But frankly, I don't even need to include that business line to justify the current valuation.

Tesla's market capitalization is $55B (AKA what the company is worth in the public markets), inline with Ford and GM (both around $50-60B). Ford and GM sell millions of cars per year, Tesla sold 103K in 2017. Ford and GM are profitable and trade at less than 0.5X 2017 sales. Tesla trades at 5X 2017 sales.

Most skeptics point out how this makes utterly no sense. I think it makes perfect sense. Fair warning, I'm about to finance-nerd out a little.

This is how I see it all playing out (and keep in mind this is probably crazy wrong).

Tesla is on track to sell its cars significantly more profitably than any other automaker (made by robots, cheaper/better batteries). This will add hundreds of incremental basis points to is gross margin relative to every other car company.

Additionally, nobody else has begun to replicate Tesla's direct to consumer, Apple-esque, retail model. At scale, this revolutionary distribution approach will add hundreds of incremental basis points in operating leverage to the company's SG&A line.

Relative to the legacy dealerships and franchise inventory model that was built pre-internet, Tesla has appropriately reinvented selling cars for the new digital era.

Vertically integrating down to the consumer touchpoint is a major edge. It allows Tesla to control the purchasing experience all the way to the last drop. An essential element of any luxury brand. Tesla is already one of the world's most successful retailers in terms of sales per square foot (in the ballpark of Apple & Tiffany's). And they haven't even started selling their most popular product yet, the Model 3. Wait until that hits scale.

The unit economics of Tesla's business will start to get, really, really fun.

This is the biggest flaw in pointing out Tesla's glaring losses and assuming they will last in perpetuity. The company isn't built to be profitable selling 100K cars per year, they have designed their business model and infrastructure (stores, superchargers, service centers) to support millions of cars on the road. If these sales never materialize the business model will flop completely, if they do, we will see enormous operating leverage where revenue growth dwarfs expense growth over the next 5 years.

Moving to the next line of the income statement. Tesla's R&D expenses are massively inflated (relative to my projections for the long-term norm) at this point in their business model. They are still so early in launching vehicles and products, that we don't have a good grasp of what is being used to fund improving existing vehicles (the Model S & X) and what is being used to develop everything else. With so much in the works that isn't being sold yet (Model 3, Semi, Model Y, etc), current R&D expenses are grossly inflated on a percentage of revenue basis.

My stance is - In the long-term, the culmination of these

factors will drive gross margins of 30% and operating margins of 10%+ in Tesla's automotive business.

If Tesla fulfills its vision and launches Model S, Model X, Model 3, Model Y, Roadster 2, The Semi and the Model P (pickup), I think the company could be selling 3 million cars in 2024, at an average price point of $65,000.

That would equate to $195B in revenue, $58.5B in gross profit, and $19.5B in operating income. Slap a 10X multiple on those earnings and you have a car business worth $195B, or about 3.5X more than today's valuation of $55B.

That's where I think we can get in 6 years, with great execution.

And this valuation includes nothing about solar roofs (the ones that already have a year-long waitlist), massive solar farms (like the one powering Kauai), or massive batteries (like the one installed in Southern Australia).

Oh, and this thing called the Tesla Network that is like Uber without a driver (self-driving Tesla robot taxis), which some analysts think is another trillion dollar opportunity.

So that's why Tesla being worth as much as GM or Ford makes sense to me. They've publicly laid out a business plan that will create a company multiples the size of these automakers.

Another factor at play is Tesla's impending success and market share gains are being priced into the market. GM and Ford are selling a lot of cars now, but that's before they start to compete head on with Tesla. The market is forward looking and realizes these earnings streams will take a massive hit, and is therefore discounting the P/E multiples of legacy automakers appropriately.

This is the Apple of the auto world. And the iPhone (Model 3) hasn't even launched yet.

Eventually, I think Tesla will use its battery technology to build planes, boats, delivery drones, and so much more. Buying equity in the company is like owning a call option on Elon Musk's inventions with no expiration. He's only 46. We are so early in seeing this vision play out.

I can't wait to see what Tesla looks like in 25 years.

The Investment Risk

Simply put, Tesla is a risky investment. The company

is burning a lot of money per quarter, has a significant amount of debt and isn't likely to produce significant free cash flow for a few years.

For this reason, Tesla is heavily reliant on raising money from the capital markets to fund its ongoing operations. This is fine in happy times, but a death sentence in an '08 scenario.

The real question is can Tesla this pull this off before some shit hits the fan. I think they can. And in their back pocket are investors like Sergey Brin, Larry Page, Ron Baron, Tencent & more, who I have a feeling would be more than willing to invest in a do or die scenario.

Either way, it's important to note that this is not a sure thing. Both bankruptcy and becoming the world's largest automaker are closer than ever.

Amazon

Jeff Bezos' empire is a financial arbitrage machine. The Seattle tech giant is pioneering an entirely new style of running a public corporation.

Despite being worth over half a trillion US Dollars, and growing revenue to over $200B in 2018, Amazon has never made a substantial profit. And as a result, nor has it paid any notable income taxes to speak of.

What's frightening, is that not a single one of Amazon's competitors enjoys this luxury.

Walmart, Costco, Target, and the rest of 'em are required to show positive earnings and pay shareholders cold-hard cash in the form of a dividend each quarter. Amazon has none of this friction, and chooses to forgo profits, so they can sell you stuff cheaper than anybody else. That's why they are taking so much market share and seem impossible to stop.

Whether this represents a permanent inflection point in investors ability to value vision over profits, or is an ephemeral phenomena propped up by historically low interest rates, is yet to be seen.

Regardless, this is one of the most important case studies in both business and financial history (along with Tesla).

Amazon has access to unlimited capital at unbeatable prices, and they aren't afraid to use it.

The goal of most businesses is to launch a product, make money from it, and return that money to investors. Amazon's goal seems far different, it's global domination. No industry is safe. Growth at all costs. Just keep getting bigger.

Valuation metrics that built the career of Warren Buffett fall by the wayside to the seemingly irrational rise in Amazon's market value. Bezos has rattled the very core of investors perception of valuation.

How has he gotten away with this?

Bezos has built remarkable trust with his investors. Amazon shareholders blindly accept that any market Amazon chooses to enter will inevitably be conquered. Just by announcing an entrance into an industry, competing stocks begin to suffer.

It's become a self-fulfilling prophecy.

Amazon says they want to enter a market, then their share price rises. They leverage that rising share price to hire top talent, and convince the market of their impending success. Although this seems crazy, it has quite a bit of merit.

The company has gone from online bookstore, to monopolizing ecommerce, to accumulating 90M+ Prime memberships, to running the world's largest cloud computing service (AWS), and soon to be dominating the world of physical retail as well (see purchase of Whole Foods).

Bezos fucking executes. That's it.

While Bezos' success as an entrepreneur is undeniable. Amazon has a darker side. The company has made strong commitments to renewable energy (which is great), but is also fostering an oddly dystopian future. They make consumption so easy it seems ridiculous not to buy more stuff.

As Amazon quietly builds a Netflix competitor as well, you have to ask what their vision for the future is? You're either sedated watching a screen or yelling at Alexa to deliver you more stuff. Sure it's cheaper, faster, and more efficient than ever.

But in its current form, Amazon is accelerating excess gluttony and materialism. These are the exact habits we so desperately need to reverse.

The challenge of getting you what you want, when you want it, is forcing Amazon to innovate.

The company has patented some insane futuristic logistics technologies. Drone beehives. Floating blimps that double as warehouses and drone charging/docking stations. Underground tunnels that shoot packages across our cities. Autonomous trucks and highway systems.

It's anybody's guess how this all plays out. But if there's one thing I can say for sure its that Amazon Prime will keep delivering packages faster and faster. In some ways its a race to 0.

Maybe it will take the extreme of being able to buy everything and have it appear instantaneously, to realize we never needed any of this crap in the first place.

Investing In Amazon

Go look at the first line (that's not legal disclosure) of Amazon's Q3 2017 earnings PR, it's no coincidence that

Operating Cash Flow is the first stat they choose to high-light. The trailing 12-month figure is $17.1B.

Based on a current market capitalization of $600B, that's a 35X multiple on trailing operating cash flow. This is Amazon's 'P/E ratio', and it seems pretty normal if you get over the fact that we're not talking about earnings (revenue continues to grow at 25% after all).

Amazon is selling a story of *compounding earnings power*.

The perception that they could be massively profitable at a moment's notice is how they get away with it.

Instead of making $17B this year and keeping it in the bank, we are reinvesting it as fast as possible so we can make $22B next year.

If the market keeps buying into this psychology (I think they will if Amazon keeps growing), it's easy to extrapo-late how the company's valuation suprasses $1T in the next few years.

Between ecommerce (still under 10% of total retail sales), physical retail (Whole Foods + no more lines = domination), AWS (AI, robots, are data monsters), Amazon has exposure to a trifecta of tailwinds that will propel growth across its core businesses for the fore-seeable future (3+ years).

Amazon is on pace to hit $20B+ in operating cash flow in 2018. By 2020 they could be well past $30B. As it becomes clear operating cash flow will surpass $30B and still has significant growth ahead, Amazon's market capitalization will hit $1T assuming the market can continue justifying a 30X+ operating cash flow multiple.

I can't see what's going to stop Amazon. Sure maybe regulation will eventually break up the company, but it's anybody's guess if that will be able to stop the growth machine Bezos has created.

Amazon doesn't really make a profit in the normal sense of the word, but their operating cash flow will get them through any recession. Amazon has $24B of cash and marketable securities on its balance sheet. They aren't going anywhere.

My gut feeling is $1T will be a cute milestone. But Amazon won't stop there. Consumption knows no limit. With Bezos at the helm, the company's moat seems to get stronger everyday. This thing could go to $5T in the next 20 years.

The achilles heel of Amazon (if there is one) is the company's stock based compensation system. This is how they hire the smartest people and incentivize them to work harder than the competition. With a stock price that's always rising this is a beautiful system. If the narrative on Amazon changes and a falling share price makes employees think twice about the value of their equity compensation, things could get dicey. Stock based compensation for the trailing 12 months ending September 2017 was $3.9B+. That's about 0.7% of Amazon's market capitalization ($3.9B/$600B) and therefore doesn't really cost the company shit. If Amazon's stock gets cut in half, it goes up to 1.4% .. still not much but you get the point. It would take a mega move (like 75% down) for this to become a problem, but still, the possibility is out there.

At the end of the day a company is just a group of people. If Amazon keeps its ability to hire and motivate the world's smartest engineers and employees, it will keep winning. If for some reason their system stops working, it will be the start of the company's downfall.

Investing

Why Invest? Why Care?

There are two main factors behind a decision to invest. The first is obvious, to make a return on your investment (aka make money). The second is rarer, but far more powerful, because you want to see something happen in the world.

In a best case scenario, you are getting involved for both.

Money is magic. The bridge that takes an invention from idea to reality.

Cities can be built, diseases can be cured, new technologies can be commercialized, people can be motivated and art can be born. It makes the impossible possible.

It gets a bad rap, but as a tool, currency is an essential part of our world, and perhaps one of civilization's greatest inventions.

The phrase *putting money to work* doesn't get enough play.

Your wealth can sit nascent in a savings account at Bank of America or you can invest in companies who have products and ideas that you believe in.

The future is an open book waiting to be written. Start writing (investing).

What is possible for humanity to achieve over the next 50 years is limited only by our collective imagination.

I implore you to leverage your capital to advance the future you want to live in.

Where you invest your money matters.

Wall St (The Business of Putting People In Business)

Yes the corporate culture of Wall St is destructive, toxic and I fucking hate bankers. But the service they provide is in many ways the most important pillar of our society.

Financial engineering is a science that rarely gets discussed or appreciated.

Remember; *money is magic.*
Elon Musk, Jeff Bezos, Steve Jobs and countless other world-class innovators have leveraged this system to commercialize their revolutionary ideas. This isn't a coincidence.

The business of putting people in business isn't going away.

And the great news is the bad guys are getting disrupted. Fintech startups like Robinhood, Wealthfront, Stripe, Square, etc have been knocking at the door for years and are only gaining more traction. These companies are empowering people like us.

Beyond startup disruption, blockchain is about to disrupt all the back office Wall St bullshit more than you could ever imagine :)

Starting a company, getting funding, and building your vision is getting easier everyday. This is the service 'Wall St' provides. Whether its an asshole in a suit (past) or a piece of software (future), every entrepreneur needs Wall St.

As an individual investor, you are a critical piece of this ecosystem.
You're at the end of the line. The lifecycle of a company's ownership goes from entrepreneur, to the suits, to the public.

We might be the smallest fish, but in many ways were

at the top of the food chain. If we don't bite, nobody's getting paid.

You're Already An Economist

Every cup of coffee you buy is a big deal.

Think about the company behind that product. The supply chain that got it to you. The farmer who grew the beans. The barista who foamed your milk. The cow that gave the milk. The farmer who took care of the cow. The trucking company that made the logistics happen.

What are the values of the enterprises you are supporting?

Are they focused on improving sustainability across thier business, or improving profit, or both?

What is their *Why*?

The economic intricacies of your morning latte are so complex that careers are built off of them (Howard Shultz), and billions are made (Starbucks). Every time you go to Starbucks you're investing in growing their business or returning capital to their shareholders. Think through these consequences.

You are already an economist. Every purchase you make is a subconsciously calculated equation to maximize some balance between short and long term happiness.

Own that. Start reverse engineering your own purchasing decisions.

Why did I get Starbucks even though I love the cafe down the street?

It was closer, faster, slightly cheaper and I didn't need to have that awkward conversation with the barista.

There are miles of insight from every move you make. Start analyzing. The intuition surrounding your purchasing decisions is the best way of understanding a company, product or service.

Be The Customer

To win at investing, you need to be an expert in the business you're investing in.

The easiest way to do this, is invest in the things you're already an expert in.

These are most likely the companies that sell the products and services you use everyday.

For instance, if you buy things on Amazon regularly you know how great of a retailer it is. If the day ever comes where you find yourself shopping on Walmart's revamped ecommerce platform, you know the competitive landscape is changing.

Another example. I used to love Chipotle. It was my favorite restaurant and I would walk 25 minutes away to wait in line 10 minutes to get a burrito. And it was so worth it. Now there is a Chipotle less than a 2 minute walk from my apartment, with no line (ever), and I have not gone in months. The guac is brown. The quality has fallen off a cliff. It's no coincidence Chipotle's share price has suffered a similar fate.

A company's greatest asset is its customers. If you are one of them, and can feel this bond getting stronger or weaker, that is a powerful clue about the direction of the business.

If the day comes where the electric car of my dreams is no longer a Tesla, it will be time to question my entire investment thesis.

Mentors

Find a mentor who has done what you're trying to do. This is true for everything, and especially investing.

All the books you read, trades you make and classes you take, will make a negligible impact on your investing acumen relative to great mentorship.

Finding a mentor isn't easy. Especially if you have no industry connections or experience.

Just start asking. Don't stop till you find one. If you're really hungry then start publishing investment research. Blogs, reports, podcasts, videos, books, whatever floats your boat. If you show enough hustle, progress and talent, a mentor might just come to you.

I've had 5 mentors in my investing career, and every single one has been priceless. There's no question I owe the bulk of my investing success to them.

This Isn't Buffett's Stock Market

Warren Buffett grew up investing in a different era. What got him to where he's at will not get you to where you want to be.

The internet has made it exponentially faster to research any company or trend. Within seconds of Googling, every public company's SEC filings are at your fingertips.

Reading the *Intelligent Investor* and studying the valuation methods of Benjamin Graham are important building blocks of understanding today's markets, but fail to answer the pressing questions of modern finance.

The P/E ratio and book value are a joke these days (although they are important to understand). These simplistic lenses of analysis cannot begin to accurately assess the value of today's most influential companies.

Firms are being run differently, the internet exists, and so does this thing called software.

Take advantage of this. Tweets, Instagram comments, Reddit threads, Snaps, are all avenues of understanding today's biggest companies and their customers.

There is a wealth of information at your fingertips accessible in seconds. This is the new frontier of DD.

Financial statements are lagging indicators of purchasing decisions.

Social media engagement is a leading indicator of purchasing decisions.

Things get really fun when the market is driving looking in the rear view mirror and you're not.

Social Media Data Is The Most Underrated DD On Wall St

At least for now. We still probably have a couple years before this really goes mainstream.

It's not just amount of followers anymore. It's engagement, and organic engagement at that. Knowing what brands are paying for distribution, and which brands are getting distribution from their customers is huge.

It's the clearest indicator of what companies are desperate, and which are not.

No matter what company or sector you're investing in, somewhere on the internet is a really valuable piece of research that most people aren't looking at. Just gotta start digging.

No Shortcuts

Investing isn't for everybody. If you don't want to put in

your 10,000+ hours you won't be good. It's like anything in life.

For some reason, because everybody needs to make money, everybody thinks they need to learn how to invest. And while I'm all for people learning, the bulk of the time it's as a side-hustle. Everybody's trying to get rich quick. That never works.

The amount of times I hear people hyping up some oil stock, high-tech chip company, or anything in an industry they don't understand is baffling.
It's frustrating as fuck.

You're not going to make a quick buck by investing in some shit your homie or colleague told you to buy because it's a 'hot' stock or cryptoasset. And if you do, you're not smart, you're lucky. That's not investing. That's gambling.

Do your own homework. Go to sec.gov and start reading filings. You will be the 1%.

SEC filings are the first principles of finance. Reading and understanding them thoroughly is the best research you can do on any company.

Work, work, work, work. That's the secret to being a great investor.

DD = Due Diligence. Wall St slang for doing enough homework on a company to convince most people in the room you know what you're talking about.

Do your DD.

Oh, and one more thing.

Everybody wants to be rich without doing shit. When you invest, most of the time your battling the smartest minds in the world with access to magnitudes more resources than you. If you think beating them is easy, you're in for a rude awakening.

Breaking Down An Investment

1. The Business

What does this company do? What are they selling? How do they make money?

What's the product?

Is it good? Are customers happy? Is this something that

will be around for the next decade? Is it getting more or less relevant by the day?

Understanding a company in and out is the most important part of investing. Before diving into the financials, you've got to know what you're looking at.

The best way to do this is to either be a customer or know a customer.

Starbucks sells coffee. Tesla sells electric cars. Apple sells iPhones.

Figure out what a company does, and if they are good at it.

You will have to be an expert on the business to have an edge investing over the broader market.

2. Leadership

"The most important metric any company has will not be found on its balance sheet, income statement or cash flows; it's leadership."

-Sam

Strategic decisions, company culture, what moves to

make when shit hits the fan (a recession) all rest on the shoulders of leadership.

It's amazing how little research or coverage is done on a CEO's background. A track record of big wins or losses can tell you a lot about what to expect. If there's one pattern I've seen, its that winning CEOs keep winning, and losing CEOs keep losing.

Beyond a track record, the most important thing to understand about leadership is what their incentives are.

Aligning incentives between shareholders and management is critical to the long-term success of any business.

The simplest way to achieve this is have the CEO own a lot of stock.

For instance. Elon Musk takes no salary from Tesla, but owns a multi-billion dollar stake in the company's common stock. When I buy a share of Tesla, I'm buying the same asset that Elon Musk has chosen to allocate the bulk of his net worth to (other than SpaceX). I fuck with that. His motivation is to create long-term value for shareholders (aka innovate), because he is one.

Contrast that with the incentives of the CEOs of other major US automakers. They are not the founders, and are paid multi-million dollar salaries that often dwarf their positions in the company's common stock. Their motivation is to keep the status quo and collect pay-checks (aka stagnate).

Do your homework on the CEO and figure out what their goals are.

(hint: most of them want to take as little risk as possible and retire rich, contrast that with Elon Musk who wants to transition the world off fossil fuels)

Guess who I'm betting on to build the future.

3. Revenue

The top of every financial statement starts with revenue. How much money does the business bring in, before accounting for any costs.

The more a company brings in, the more that can potentially flow to the bottom line. That is why consis-tent growth is often a valid excuse for a lack of profit-ability, at least in this market (see Amazon).

This is the most basic, and the first financial metric to understand.

How many widgets is this company selling, and how much revenue is that bringing in?

Is it up (business is growing) or down (business is shrinking) from last year?

4. Earnings (aka Profit)

Revenue is great. And a lot of it, growing fast, is really great ... but that's just the first test. Now we're getting deeper :)

Are they profitable?

Everybody's overthinking financials. Sure, financial statements have a million lines and look really complicated, but when you boil things down, it gets pretty simple.

Businesses have two states. Cash producing or cash burning.

Producing cash isn't necessarily a good thing and burning cash isn't necessarily a bad thing.

There are millions of reasons why a company could be losing money. Maybe it's just a crappy business that isn't providing any value. Maybe management is thinking long-term and sacrificing near-term profits to build a moat.

As a general rule of thumb, startups burn capital because they are investing in the future (growth) and mature companies generate cash because they are paying back the past (investors).

The metric I personally track to gauge profitability is *EBIT* (aka Earnings Before Interest or Taxes), sometimes referred to as Operating Income.

EBIT tells me if the company made money or not in a given period. In my opinion, it's the closest thing to the core earnings of the business.

There are a lot of other metrics that constitute Wall St slang for profit; EBITDA, Net Income, NOPAT, etc. They are all slightly different and it would take me hours to explain the nuances that makeup each one. But across the board, the gist is the same. They will tell you if the business made or lost money, AKA the business's *earnings*.

For simplicity, my rule of thumb is to pick one and use it for every business you analyze. At least that will make it consistent.

Tesla's EBIT is negative. The company is on track to post an operating loss (EBIT) of about -$1.5B in 2017.

You might be wondering how a company could be worth $50B+, if it is losing $1.5B per year?

Here's my reasoning. Tesla is in startup mode. I'm ok with Tesla making no profit today because I think they are investing to generate significant profits in the future.

This is a great example of why glancing at the profit of a business in one year is only scratching the surface.

It's fundamental to understand whether a business is making or losing money at a moment in time. But the trajectory of that profit or loss trend, is the true determinant of value.

5. Valuation (Predicting The Future)

So now we have a basic understanding of what a company does, how much money it's bringing in, and how much of that is flowing to the bottomline.

Now it's time to figure out what to pay for it.

This is the really, really hard part that Nobel prizes are given out for because no one knows what the answer is.

The most commonly accepted framework to gauge a company's valuation is the P/E (Price/Earnings) ratio. This will tell you the multiple you are paying for a company's annual profits.

If Firm ABC is trading at $20 per share (price), and it earned $1 per share (earnings), it's P/E ratio is 20X (price/earnings). It may sound tricky at first, but it's pretty straightforward.

Historically, the S&P 500 (and index of the 500 largest publicly traded US companies) trades at a P/E ratio of 15-20X. From January 1971 to June 2017, the S&P 500 averaged a P/E ratio of 19.4X [11]. Most people accept this as the standard, or what a normal valuation should be.

Let's think about that for a second. On average, the market values businesses at 19.4 times the profit they generate in a single year.

Extrapolating this methodology, if your lemonade stand

generates $500 in profit per year, it would be worth $9,700 at a P/E ratio of 19.4X.

Now one might rationally conclude that any business trading at a P/E ratio higher than 19.4X is overvalued, and any business trading at a P/E ratio below 19.4X is undervalued. Unfortunately, it's not that simple.

Remember, at a P/E ratio of 19.4X, you're paying for almost 20 years worth of profits. That's a long time.

What would you rather own?

Lemonade Stand A that is doing $0 in profit this year, but $1,000 next year and $2,000 the year after that?

OR

Lemonade Stand B that is doing $500 in profit this year, $500 next year and will continue to earn $500 in perpetuity.

In the first scenario (Lemonade Stand A) you would accumulate $3,000 in earnings after 3 years. In the second scenario (Lemonade Stand B) you would accumulate $1,500 in the same period. This illustrates the importance of future earnings trajectory over current earnings.

Future earnings far outweigh current earnings, and past earnings are almost irrelevant. Just because a business is profitable today, doesn't mean it will be tomorrow.

To help better rationalize my personal investments, I use a back of the napkin formula I call *Years To Payback* (YTP). How many years would it take for a company to return the entire value of my investment in profit?

Let's say both Lemonade Stand A & B (from the scenario above) are trading at a price of $3,000. The YTP of Lemonade Stand A is 3 years and the YTP of Lemonade Stand B is 6 years. If my assumptions about the trajectory of their future profits are correct, I would say Lemonade Stand A is a far better investment, despite having much lower current earnings.

All of this is guesswork. There are far more granular ways to calculate the value of companies, like discounted cash flow models (DCFs) for instance. But they all boil down to the same thing.

It's Art, Not Science

Stocks are stories.

The hard part isn't calculating the P/E Ratio, YTP or making a DCF... The hard part is accurately forecasting how the market's perception of those future financial scenarios will change. It's fucking meta.

If you really want to be a master at financial markets, you have to be a master at human psychology.

You're not guessing what assets are worth. You're guessing what people will guess assets are worth in the future.

The most intense number crunching on Wall St is a manifestation of covering up insecurities related to this perplexing question; what is a company worth?

Nobody can accurately model a company's financials 5 years into the future.

The crux is that people buy products. And you can't model people.

Business Is Art

Businesses have the power to affect millions of people and profoundly impact the course of society.

The most complex form of art is a corporation. You're building the machine that makes the machine (yeah I stole this from Elon Musk).

Every business is a movement to accomplish a goal.

It is as cross disciplinary as possible. Truly a renaissance man's endeavor. Orchestrating groups of people to accomplish a mission in harmony. This is how global progress happens.

Much like art, passion is the most important part of business. If you are not deeply inspired and motivated your chances of greatness are slim.

As a founder you're guiding inspiration at every turn.

Elon Musk's engineering smarts, understanding of physics, charisma, are all legendary, but I'd argue they have nothing on his creativity. At his core, in many ways he is an artist. The only thing up for debate is whether Tesla or SpaceX will be his *piece de resistance*.

Never Stop Learning

The best investing theories, formulas and philosophies have yet to be discovered.

The day you think you know it all, is the day you lose.

This is why cryptoassets are so fascinating. Nobel prizes are waiting to be claimed.

This book should leave you with more questions than answers.

Get used to it, that's what investing feels like.

Entrepreneurship

This part was tricky to write because although I'm trying to be an entrepreneur I haven't been successful yet. I'm young and have a lot to learn. But I have a weird feeling now is a historically unique time for entrepreneurship. So I want to share the philosophies that guide me.

Anything Is Possible

"This my life, homie you decide yours."
        -Kanye West

There has never been a better time to be alive. I mean it. Like really.

This cannot be understated.

Don't get fooled by political turmoil, depressing headlines or your homies negativity.

The internet at scale is commoditizing the ability to change the world and acquire life changing wealth, for everyone.

Following your passion and reaching your dreams has never been easier.

I don't care what you want to be or do. It's possible.

As far as I can tell, the closest thing there is to a formula is something like this:

Hard work + patience + a stubborn (and accurate) vision =
success

Go to Google and you can start learning how to do any-thing immediately.

Libraries and textbooks are no longer the gatekeepers of knowledge, your hustle is.

You could literally start mastering any skill tomorrow if you have access to the internet.

Beyond acquiring knowledge, buying tools and supplies is easier and cheaper than ever.

Amazon, the world's everything store, is selling exactly what you need to prototype anything and will deliver it in 2 days at an unbeatable price with just the click of a button.

YouTube + a smartphone and you can launch your own TV show that is immediately distributed across the entire planet.

Instagram isn't just for models. Start posting your art, products, passion and you can build a fanbase, and begin to craft a monetizable following around your work.

Twitter gives your voice a megaphone to share ideas

on politics, sports, technology or anything, around the world, instantly.

These are all tools that have never existed before and give entrepreneurs incredible power. This should not be taken lightly.

More than ever before, our imagination is the only limiting factor to what we can achieve.

Be Enlightened

"Who the Hell are you and what the Hell is that?"
        -Chris Reed

Every great business starts with no guap and no believers.

Arguably the hardest part of entrepreneurship is being enlightened.

Enlightened (per my definition) is believing in your idea before anyone else does.

You have to be your first fan. If you're not, nobody will be.

When I put out my first YouTube video on HyperChange it was a bittersweet moment. A couple people liked it, but the overwhelming response from people I admired was that it was a huge mistake.

My mentors, who were a lot smarter, more successful and experienced, did not see the vision. The stubborn anarchist in me used this to add fuel to the fire. I saw the potential.

Family, friends and the world will probably think you are crazy when you go all in on your idea. Especially if it's your first real power move. AKA some life shit you do on your own volition.

Is that a scary concept? Sure. It's why most people never start businesses.

Failing

"You don't fail when you fail"
        -Chris Reed

Why the fuck is everybody scared of failing? Failing is such a bad word. It should be reframed as learning.
I've tried to start so many companies that just flopped. When I was 14, I made limited edition duct-tape wallets

and tried to sell them online (my first ecommerce project, colorwallets.com). Didn't even sell a single one. But I learned how to build a website and realized that I could start my own thing.

Society counts that as a failure. I count it as the first crucial building block of my entrepreneurial DNA.

A few streetwear brands, a penny stock newsletter, a hydroponic farming company, a 3d printed trinket business, a finance news app, an online record label ... the amount of things I've started that have failed is epic. Really my life is just a track record of one crappy startup idea after the next.

But.

All those hours, experiences and 'wasted' dollars (thousands) are turning out to be priceless.

Each 'failure' taught me a lesson. Piece by piece, failure by failure, I taught myself how to be an entrepreneur.

Failure is an essential element of success. You won't get anywhere without it.

Regret Minimization Framework

This chapter title and philosophy is 100% copied from Jeff Bezos. He mentioned this mentality in a talk as his reason for starting Amazon, and it's been one of my mantras ever since.

The basic idea is to take a step back and imagine that you are 80 years old reflecting on your life. You want to minimize the regrets you have. Asking that girl you like out, following that crazy gut feeling to start a company, traveling the world ... whatever it is.

We only get one shot at this thing called life, and it's worth thinking about what you want to do with it. Perhaps the scariest thing about life is realizing that it's exactly what you make of it. Free will is real.

Stop living for your resume. Start living for your legacy.

For me, not trying is so much scarier than failing.

Knowing that you have the chance (no matter how small) to make an impact, follow your dream, and be an entrepreneur and not giving it a shot? Nah ... I'm doing it.

There is only one thing scarier than my family and friends

thinking I'm a loser because my dumb idea flopped. It's being 80 years old and realizing that fear of failure was what held me back from trying to do what I love.

Hustle & Positivity

You can't control how many times you will get knocked down. But you can control the amount of times you get back up.

Nothing is easy. A flip, passive income, a lick, whatever you want to call your get rich quick scheme is BS.

At the beginning you need to be resourceful, scrappy and work your ass off. Hustle is key. So is positivity.

Entrepreneurship is one setback and failure after the next. Everything takes twice as long and and costs twice as much as you think.

Just keep your head up and keep hustling. The second you stop, you lose.

Fuck The Money

"When you're young you spend time to get money, when you're old you spend money to get time" *(or something like that)*

   -GaryVee

Money is a tool. I don't want money. I want to do what I want to do. Money helps with that.

The amount of my friends who work 9-5s that they are not passionate about or inspired by, makes me really sad. Sure, most of them are making six-figures, buying fancy food, taking dope trips and seem happy.

But I can't help feel like there's an emptiness behind it.

There's one thing money cannot buy. That's time.

If you're under 30 and don't have a family you should be taking as much risk as possible. Chasing your dreams and failing (learning) seems like a win/win. You will never get this shot again. You can always take the corporate job later.

Cubicles aren't going anywhere. Your chance to change the world might be.

Honesty & Integrity

It takes a lifetime to build a reputation, but only a moment to ruin one.

In elementary school I stole Jesse Clurman's (Jclur) Charizard. I remember the moment like it was yesterday. It was a Friday night and my parents and I were leaving the Clurman's after an epic dinner party. Jclur and I had been playing Pokemon all night in his room, and I had forgotten my socks upstairs. Everybody was near the door while I ran back up to grab them. Then I saw it glimmering out of the corner of my eye.

Holographic Charizard. The holy grail of Pokemon cards at the time. I slipped it in my pocket and took it with me. The high didn't last. Right after we got home the Clurmans already were calling asking if I'd seen Jclur's card ... I caved quickly and had to write a note apologizing to Jclur the next day and give him Charizard back. We've been childhood best friends since day 1, so we got over it pretty quick. But I'll never forget that feeling of guilt.

I'm not exactly sure why that stuck with me, but I feel lucky to have learned this lesson early.

Be honest. Have integrity. Do the right thing. The truth will always win.

It's much better to try with good intentions and fail, than win by sacrificing your morals. I hope you don't have to learn that the hard way.

Elon Musk

Elon Musk is redefining what's possible for a single entrepreneur.

Einstein, Jobs, Da Vinci, Musk, are all artists in their own way.

Musk might be the best of the bunch. What he's doing with SpaceX, Tesla, Neuralink, The Boring Company, etc ...

If he pulls all this off - Elon's companies will bring exceptional value to humanity, and change the world, but I don't they will be his greatest gifts.
Inspiration will be.

Proving that anything is possible. No dream is too big too accomplish.

The wave of entrepreneurs he inspires who will take us out of this solar system and so far beyond. This might be Elon's greatest gift.

If robots and AI don't kill us, we are in for a hell of a ride, and a lot of it is thanks to this guy.

filchê

"To be filchê is filchê"
         -Tyler, filche lifestyle follower

If I ever get a tattoo, it will be *filchê*. Pronounced (fill-chee).

It's an expression of positivity, joy, individuality and creativity.

It's a word my squad made up in made up in high-school, and just owned.

Now it's a movement.

One of my best friends, and the biggest pioneer behind the filchê lifestyle still goes by jfilchê to this day. He's a legend. Gives no fucks, and is just himself. People like that go 0 to 1.

Why don't more people invent words? All the words we use today were just invented by somebody else.

There are so many unwritten rules in society that we blindly follow because it's the norm.

Tesla is filchê. You are filchê.

The world has the potential to be filchê.

Sources

[1] World Economic Forum "The New Plastics Economy"
http://www3.weforum.org/docs/WEF_The_New_Plastics_Economy.pdf

[2] The Guardian "Biologists think 50% of species will be facing extinction by the end of the century"
https://www.theguardian.com/environment/2017/feb/25/half-all-species-extinct-end-century-vatican-conference

[3] Climate Central "The Last Time CO2 Was This High, Humans Didn't Exist"
http://www.climatecentral.org/news/the-last-time-co2-was-this-high-humans-didnt-exist-15938

[4] Scientific American "2017 Was The Third Hottest Year On Record For The US"
https://www.scientificamerican.com/article/2017-was-the-third-hottest-year-on-record-for-the-u-s/

[5] National Geographic "Rainforests"
https://www.nationalgeographic.com/environment/habitats/rain-forests/

[6] National Geographic "Deforestation"

https://www.nationalgeographic.com/environment/
global-warming/deforestation/

[7] NASA "Climate Change: How Do We Know?"
https://climate.nasa.gov/evidence/

[8] Salon "America is a wasteland: The U.S. produces a shock-
ing amount of garbage"
https://www.salon.com/2016/07/15/america_is_a_wasteland_
the_u_s_produces_a_shocking_amount_of_garbage_partner/

[9] SpaceX Website
http://www.spacex.com/

[10] Recode "Look what happened to grocery stocks after
Amazon announced it's buying Whole Foods"
https://www.recode.net/2017/6/16/15819996/
amazon-whole-foods-acquisition-supermarket-stock-price

[11] Valuescope "The S&P 500 P/E Ratio: A Historical
Perspective"
www.valuescopeinc.com/resources/white-papers/
the-sp-500-pe-ratio-a-historical-perspective/

28995326R00070

Printed in Great Britain
by Amazon